I0017181

Luc Thibert

Create a successful blog.

Luc Thibert
Create a successful blog

Original edition : Saint-Hubert, PQ, 2024
Published in collaboration with Blurb éditions

U.S. edition on Amazon.com

Cover design: Gerd Altmann
Layout: BookWright
Note - Self-publishing implies that spelling mistakes may creep into the texts. Please be indulgent and communicate them, for possible corrections on future editions, to the following e-mail address: luc.thibert1961@gmail.com

Printed in the U.S.A.
under the supervision of Blurb
Blurb, Inc. PO Box 728, San Francisco, CA 94104-0728
©2024 Blurb. All rights reserved.

The first thing you need to decide when creating your blog is what you want to achieve with it, and what it can do if it succeeds.

- Ron Dawson

Preface

Creating a successful blog

Setting up a blog can be an exciting and rewarding adventure. This book is a comprehensive, step-by-step guide to creating and running a successful blog, focusing on quality content, effective promotion and eventually smart monetization. You know what, it's a great time to get involved in serious blogging. Getting into blogging today remains an excellent opportunity due to the continued growth of the Internet, demand for content, easy access to tools and technologies, diverse monetization opportunities, community support, creative flexibility and benefits in terms of personal and professional development. By exploiting these advantages, you can create a blog that not only succeeds, but also brings you satisfaction and fulfillment.

Getting started in blogging is an adventure full of possibilities. With passion, patience and perseverance, you can create a blog that not only reflects your vision, but also resonates with a wide audience. Believe in yourself, stay authentic and continue to learn and evolve along the way. The journey can sometimes be difficult, but it's also incredibly rewarding.

Good luck and, above all, happy blogging!

Luc Thibert

What's on the menu?

Chapter 1: Introduction

- What is a blog?
- The benefits of having a blog.
- The different blog platforms

Chapter 2: Choosing your niche

- Identify your passions and skills.
- Analyze the competition.
- Find a profitable and unique niche.

Chapter 3: Laying the foundations

 - Choose a domain name.
- Select a web host.
- Install and configure blog platform (WordPress, Wix).

Chapter 4: Creating quality content

- Find article ideas.
- Write captivating and informative articles.
- Use media (images, videos) effectively.

Chapter 5: Optimizing for search engines

- Understand the basics of search engine optimization (SEO).
- Use the right keywords.
- Optimize site structure for SEO.

Chapter 6: Promoting your blog

- Use social networks to promote your articles.
- Collaborate with other bloggers.
- Use e-mail marketing to build reader loyalty.

Chapter 7: Monetize your blog

- Different ways to earn money with a blog.
(Advertising, affiliate marketing, digital products, etc.)
- Developing an effective monetization strategy.
- Mistakes to avoid when monetizing.

Chapter 8: Managing and growing your blog.

- Analyze traffic statistics.
- Respond to reader comments and e-mails.
- Update content regularly.
- Evolve with blogging trends.

Chapter 9: Overcoming obstacles.

- Dealing with lack of motivation.
- Dealing with criticism and negative feedback.
- Keep a long-term vision.

Chapter 10: Conclusion

- Recap of key points.
- Encouragement and advice for the future.

Chapter 1 : Introduction

➢ What is a blog?

A blog is a type of website where content is usually presented in the form of articles or blog posts published on a regular basis and organized chronologically. These articles can cover a wide range of subjects, from news and trends to more personal or specialized topics. Blogs are often run by individuals or groups who share their knowledge, experience, opinions or passions with their audience. Readers can interact with the content by leaving comments, which often creates a community around the blog. Blogs can be used for personal, professional, educational or business purposes, and have become a popular way for people to express themselves online and share their expertise with the world.

➢Why create a blog?

A blog fulfils a number of important functions, which can vary according to the objectives of its creator. It offers many advantages, whether for individuals or businesses. Here are some of the main advantages of having a blog:

1.   Sharing information and knowledge:

Blogs are often used to share knowledge, skills, opinions, advice and analysis on specific subjects. Whether in the personal, professional, academic or leisure sphere, a blog can be used to share all kinds of information on distinctive subjects. It can also be useful for educating, informing or entertaining a targeted audience.

2.   Establish an online presence:

For individuals and businesses alike, a blog can be an effective way to establish an online presence for individuals, professionals or companies, and gain exposure in their area of expertise. It provides a dedicated platform for sharing relevant content and attracting the attention of Internet users. Publishing quality content on a regular basis can help build credibility and visibility online.

3.   Interact with an audience:
Blogs enable authors to dialogue and interact with their audience through comments and social networks. This interaction can foster reader engagement and loyalty, encourage discussion and create a community around the blog.

4.   Build authority and credibility:
By regularly publishing quality content on relevant topics, a blogger can establish credibility and become an authority in his or her field of expertise. This can lead to professional opportunities, collaborations and increased recognition.

5.   Monetization:
A blog can be used as a source of income by monetizing traffic with advertising, affiliate marketing, selling products or services, or creating sponsored content. For some professional bloggers, blogging can even become a full-time source of income.

6.   Establish professional relationships:
A blog can be used to build relationships with others in the industry or field of interest, whether by collaborating on articles, exchanging links, or participating in joint events and projects.

7.   Develop skills:
Keeping a blog can help develop many useful skills such as writing, research, content management, online marketing, social network management, etc.

8.   Improve SEO:
Blogs are well-suited for search engine optimization (SEO) as they offer a platform to publish fresh, relevant content on a regular basis. By using good SEO practices, a blog can improve its visibility in search engine results and attract more organic traffic.

9.   Personal expression:
For many people, a blog is a way to express themselves, to share their thoughts, feelings and experiences with the world. This can be therapeutic, educational or simply personally rewarding.

Overall, a blog can be a versatile and powerful tool for achieving a variety of goals, whether personal, professional or commercial. It offers a diverse range of benefits, from creating an online presence to engaging with an audience, developing skills and generating income.

➢The different blogging platforms

There are several blogging platforms that offer free options for bloggers. Here are some of the most popular platforms where you can create a blog with no upfront costs:

1. Blogger (formerly Blogspot):
Owned by Google, Blogger is one of the oldest and most popular blogging platforms. It offers free blog hosting with a subdomain such as "yourname.blogspot.com". Blogger is beginner-friendly and offers a variety of features for customizing the design and content of your blog.

2. WordPress.com:
WordPress.com is a hosted version of the WordPress content management platform. It offers free plans with a subdomain such as "yourname.wordpress.com". Although free features are limited compared to paid plans, WordPress.com remains a solid option for beginners wishing to start a blog without upfront costs.

3. Medium:
Medium is a blogging platform focused on quality content and discussion. Although Medium doesn't allow you to fully customize your blog's design, it does offer a clean layout and high visibility thanks to its community of users. You can create an account for free and start publishing articles immediately.

4. Tumblr:
Tumblr is a microblogging platform that combines blogging and social networking. It's easy to use and allows you to publish a variety of content, including text, images, videos, links and more. Tumblr offers customization options and a "yourname.tumblr.com" subdomain.

5. Wix:
Wix is primarily known for its website builder, but it also offers a blogging option. You can create a free blog with Wix using their intuitive editor and predefined templates. However, keep in mind that free features are limited and there are paid options to unlock advanced functionality.

6. Webador:
Webador may also be a good option for those looking for a simple, user-friendly platform to create a blog or website. However, if you need more advanced features or customization, you may want to explore other options. Be sure to compare features, prices and user reviews before making a decision.

➢Conclusion :

In conclusion, most of these platforms offer free solutions for starting a blog, but it's important to note that they may have limitations in terms of customization, feature evolution and control compared to paid options or self-hosting. Before choosing a platform, be sure to check their features, terms of use and scalability to ensure they meet your long-term needs. In summary, for any website creation platform, it's important to do thorough research, compare features and prices (in the event you want to upgrade your Blog), and read user reviews on forums before making a final decision.

Personally, my partner and I opted for the Wix package. First and foremost, because it was the answer to having everything under the same roof. Efficient blog creation software, domain name acquisition, hosting, SEO assistance, technical support and many other options that can be added to the project along the way. Chapter 3 will set out these facts for you in detail, so you'll be able to see just how easy and user-friendly the Wix ready-to-publish package is.

Chapter 2: Choosing your niche

Finding the right niche for your blog is crucial to its long-term success. Here are a few tips to help you identify a niche that matches your interests, skills and the needs of your target audience:

1.   Identify your passions and skills:
Start by making a list of your passions, interests and skills. What subjects are you really passionate about? In what areas do you have particular knowledge or skills? Choosing a niche that interests you and in which you excel will keep you motivated and writing with authenticity.

2.   Research demand and competition:
Once you've identified a few potential niche ideas, do some research to assess demand and competition in those areas. Use keyword research tools like Google Keyword Planner, Semrush or Ubersuggest to find out the search volume and competitiveness of keywords related to your niche. Also consult other blogs and websites in your niche to assess the competition and identify gaps you could fill.

3.   Define your target audience:
Spend some time defining your target audience in detail. Who are they? What are their needs, problems and interests? Understanding your target audience will help you tailor your content to meet their needs and grab their attention.

4.   Find a unique angle:
Try to find a unique angle or original perspective on your niche that will set you apart from the competition. This could be a unique approach to the subject, a distinctive writing style, or a particular expertise you bring to the topic.

5.   Assess the potential for profitability:
In addition to personal interest, also think about the profit potential of your niche. Explore different ways of monetizing your blog in this niche, whether through advertising, affiliate marketing, selling products or services, etc.

6.   Stay flexible and open to feedback:
Keep in mind that your niche may evolve over time based on your interests, market trends and feedback from your audience. Stay flexible and open to adjustments as you learn and grow as a blogger.

By following these tips, you'll be better equipped to find the ideal niche for your blog and get off to a good start. Get started!

Chapter 3: Laying the foundations

Choosing a domain name:

A domain name is the unique address that identifies a website on the Internet. It's what users type into their browser's address bar to access a specific website. For example, in the address "www.google.com", "google.com" is the domain name.

➢**Here are some key points to understand about domain names :**

1.   Structure of a domain name :

- Main name :
The main part of the domain name, such as "google" in "google.com".

- Domain extension :
The part following the dot, such as ".com", ".org", ".net", etc. Extensions can indicate the type of site (commercial, non-profit, network, etc.) or the country of origin (such as ".fr" for France, ".uk" for the UK, ".ca" for Canada, etc.).

2.   How it works :
Just for information, domain names serve as a user-friendly substitute for IP addresses, which are series of numbers used by computers to identify servers on the Internet. For example, Google's IP address might be something like "172.217.10.46", but it's much easier to remember "google.com".

3.   Registration :
To use a domain name, you must reserve it by registering it with a domain name registrar. This process usually involves paying an annual fee to retain the right to use the domain name.

4. Choosing a domain name :

A good domain name should be short, easy to remember, and representative of your brand or content. It's also important to check that the desired domain name is available and not already registered by someone else.

5. Examples of common domain extensions :

- .com: Used mainly for commercial sites, but widely used by all kinds of sites.
- .org: Generally used by non-profit organizations.
- .net: Initially intended for networks, but used by various types of sites.
- .edu: Used by educational institutions.
- .gov: Reserved for government agencies.

In short, a domain name is an essential part of your website's online identity. It facilitates user access to your site and plays an important role in the branding and visibility of your online presence.

➤Selecting a web host :

For your website to be accessible on the Internet, you need a web host. A web host provides the infrastructure needed to store your site files and make them accessible to online users. Here are a few reasons why a web host is necessary:

1. File storage :

Your website files, including HTML pages, images, videos and databases, need to be stored on a server. A web host provides this storage space.

2. Accessibility :

A web host guarantees that your site is accessible 24/7. Web hosts use powerful, reliable servers to ensure continuous availability of your site.

3. Domain management :

Web hosts often manage the registration and renewal of domain names. Although you can purchase a domain separately, many web hosts offer integrated domain management services.

4. Technical support :

Web hosts provide technical support to help you solve any technical problems that may arise with your site. This can include server management, security issues, and performance optimizations.

5.   Additional features :

Web hosts often offer additional features such as automatic backups, SSL security, e-mail accounts associated with your domain, site creation tools, and more.

➤ **However, there are different types of web hosting for different needs :**

1.   Shared hosting :

several websites share the same server. This is an economical option, and sufficient for small blogs and websites with moderate traffic.

2.   VPS (Virtual Private Server) hosting :

Offers more resources and flexibility than shared hosting, as your site is hosted on a dedicated part of a server.

3.   Dedicated hosting :

You have an entire server to yourself. Ideal for high-traffic sites with specific performance and security requirements.

4.   Cloud hosting :

Utilizes the resources of multiple servers to balance load and maximize uptime. It's a flexible, scalable option.

5.   Website builders with integrated hosting :

Services like Wix, Squarespace, and WordPress.com include web hosting in their offering, simplifying the process for users.

In short, a web host is essential for making your site accessible on the Internet. It provides not only storage space, but also the resources and support needed to keep your site up and running.

➢ Installing and configuring the blog platform (WordPress or WIX)

Here's a general guide to the two most popular blog platforms :

1. WordPress.org

Installation on a web server :

1.   Choose a web host :
Make sure your host supports WordPress and offers easy installation.
Hosting providers like Bluehost, SiteGround, and A2 Hosting are popular for
WordPress.

2.   Download WordPress :
Go to the official WordPress website (wordpress.org) and download the
latest version of WordPress.

3.   Upload files :
Use an FTP client like FileZilla to upload WordPress files to your server in
the desired directory.

4.   Create a database :
Connect to your cPanel or your hosting provider's management interface
and create a MySQL database. Make a note of the database name, user
name and password.

5.   Set up WordPress :
- Access your domain (for example, yourdomain.com).
- Follow the on-screen instructions to configure your wp-config.php file.
Enter your database details.
- Continue installation by entering your site information (site title,
username, password, email address).

6.   Finalize the installation :
Click on "Install WordPress" and follow the final instructions.

Basic configuration :

1.   Log in to your dashboard :
Go to yourdomain.com/wp-admin and log in with your information.

2.   Choose a theme :
Go to Appearance > Themes and select a free or premium theme that suits your blog.

3.   Install essential plugins :
Go to Extensions > Add to install plugins such as Akismet (anti-spam), Yoast SEO (SEO), and Jetpack (additional features).

4.   Configure basic settings :
- Set permalinks in Settings > Permalinks to improve SEO.
- Configure reading and discussion options in Settings > Reading and Settings > Discussion.

2. Wix.com

Wix is often considered one of the most user-friendly and intuitive website creation platforms, making it an excellent option for beginners or those who prefer an all-in-one solution without having to worry about the technical aspects. Here's why Wix can be easier to use for creating and managing a blog:

1. Intuitive interface :
Wix features a highly intuitive drag-and-drop editor that lets you create and customize websites without any programming knowledge. You can add elements such as text, images, videos, forms and much more simply by dragging them onto your page.

2. Predefined templates :
Wix offers a wide selection of professional, aesthetically pleasing website and blog templates. You can choose a template that suits your style and needs, then easily customize it.

3. Built-in features :
Wix includes many built-in features, such as blogging tools, photo galleries, contact forms, and e-commerce functionality. This means you don't need to install additional plugins or extensions to get the basic functionality of your blog.

4. Hosting included :
Wix takes care of hosting your website, which means you don't have to worry about finding a separate web host. Your site is automatically hosted on Wix servers, and you benefit from their security and performance infrastructure.

5. Support and assistance :

Wix offers robust customer support and a comprehensive knowledge base with guides, tutorials and FAQs. If you run into problems or have questions, you can easily find answers or contact Wix support.

6. Easy, user-friendly configuration.

Steps to create a blog with Wix :

1. Create an account :
- Go to Wix.com and sign up using your email address or a social account.

2. Choose a template :
- After registering, you'll be prompted to choose a template. Select a blog template from the available options.

3. Customize your site :
- Use Wix's drag-and-drop editor to add and customize elements of your site. You can modify text, images, colors and layout to suit your preferences.

4. Add a blog section :
- In the Wix editor, go to the main menu, click "Add" > "Blog" and follow the instructions to add a blog section to your site.

5. Write and publish articles :
- Once you've added a blog section, click on "Create a Post" to write and publish your articles. You can add images, videos and other multimedia elements to your posts.

6. Configure settings :
- Configure your blog's settings, such as categories, tags, comments and social network sharing options.

7. Publish your site :
- When you're ready, click "Publish" to put your site online. You can use a free domain provided by Wix (votrenom.wixsite.com) or connect a custom domain if you have a paid subscription.

➢**Conclusion :**

To sum up, Wix is a very accessible option for creating and managing a blog, thanks to its user-friendly interface, predefined templates and integrated features. For those looking for a simple, hassle-free solution to get started in blogging, Wix is an excellent platform to consider. Personally, I love it. But Worldpress also enjoys a very good reputation among hardened bloggers. The choice is yours!

Chapter 4: Creating quality content

Creating quality content is essential to attracting and retaining readers on your blog. Here's a detailed guide to help you produce quality content:

➤ Know your target audience

Define your audience :
- Identify who your ideal readers are: their age, gender, profession, interests, needs and problems.

➤ Conduct in-depth research

Research the subject :
- Use reliable, up-to-date sources to gather accurate information.
- Read books, academic articles, market studies and relevant blog posts.

➤ Plan and structure your content

Create a plan :
- Clearly define the purpose of your articles: to inform, educate, entertain, etc.
- Draw up an outline or summary with the main points you want to cover.

➤ Article structure :

- Introduction :
Grab the reader's attention with an intriguing hook or question. Introduce the subject and explain why it's important.

- Article body :
Divide the content into logical sections or subheadings. Use short

paragraphs, bulleted lists and images to facilitate reading.

- Conclusion :
Summarize the article's key points. Include a call to action (CTA), encouraging readers to leave a comment, share the article, or subscribe to your newsletter.

➢Write with clarity and commitment

Clarity and conciseness :
- Write in simple, clear language. Avoid jargon and complex sentences.
- Be direct and to the point. Every sentence should add value.

Tone and style :
- Adapt your tone to your target audience. For example, use a professional tone for a business blog, or a casual tone for a lifestyle blog.
- Be authentic and show your personality through your writing.

➢Use visual elements

Images and graphics :
- Incorporate high-quality images, infographics, and relevant graphics to illustrate your points.
- Use tools like Canva or Piktochart to create eye-catching visuals.

Videos and media :
- Add explanatory videos, tutorials, or testimonials to enrich your content.
- Make sure all visual elements are optimized for the web (file size, format).

Internal and external links :
- Add internal links to other articles on your blog to keep readers on your site.
- Use external links to credible sources to reinforce your blog's reliability.

Chapter 5: Optimizing for search engines

Search engine optimization (SEO) is essential for increasing your blog's visibility and attracting more visitors. Here's a detailed guide on how to optimize your blog for search engines, along with practical tips you can apply:

➤ Keyword research

Keyword identification :
- Use tools like Google Keyword Planner, Ahrefs, Semrush, or Ubersuggest to find relevant keywords for your niche.
- Look for keywords with high search volume but low to medium competition.

Types of keywords :
- Primary keywords: Those that represent the main subject of your article.
- Secondary keywords: Variations and synonyms of your main keywords.
- Long-tail keywords: More specific, less competitive phrases that attract a targeted audience.

➤ On-page optimization

Titles and meta-descriptions :
- Include your main keywords in titles (H1 tags) and meta-descriptions.
- Keep titles attractive and meta-descriptions succinct, with a call to action.

Heading tags (H1, H2, H3) :
- Use H1 tags for main titles and H2/H3 for subtitles.
- Naturally incorporate keywords into these tags to improve structure and

readability.

User-friendly URLs :
- Create short, descriptive URLs, including relevant keywords.
- Avoid long URLs with complex parameters.

Internal and external links :
- Add internal links to other relevant articles on your blog to improve navigation and indexing.
- Use external links to reliable, relevant sources to enhance the credibility of your content.

Image optimization :
- Use descriptive file names and include words to describe them.

Chapter 6: Promoting your blog

Promoting your blog is also a crucial step in attracting readers, increasing your audience and strengthening your online presence. Here's a list of the best ways to promote your blog effectively:

➢Using social networks

Choose the right platforms :
- Identify where your target audience is (Facebook, Twitter, Instagram, LinkedIn, Pinterest, etc.) and focus your efforts on these platforms.

Share content :
- Share every new blog post on your social media profiles.
- Use attractive visuals, relevant hashtags and engaging descriptions to increase visibility.

Engagement :
- Interact with your audience by responding to comments, asking questions and participating in discussions.
- Join groups and communities related to your niche to share your content and interact with interested people.

➢Email marketing

Create a mailing list :
- Add sign-up forms to your blog to collect your readers' email addresses.

Send newsletters :
- Send regular newsletters with blog updates, exclusive content and promotions.

Segmentation :
- Segment your mailing list to send personalized, relevant messages to different groups of readers.

➢Guest blogging

Write for other blogs :
- Write guest articles for popular blogs in your niche. Include links to your own blog to attract new readers.

Invite guest bloggers :
- Invite experts or influencers to write articles for your blog. They'll probably share their contribution with their own audience, increasing your visibility.

➢SEO (Search Engine Optimization)

On-page optimization :

- Use relevant keywords in your titles, subtitles, and content.
- Optimize images with appropriate alt tags and descriptions.

Backlink building :

- Get quality links from other websites by participating in forums, submitting guest articles, and establishing partnerships.

Evergreen content :
- Create sustainable content that remains relevant and continues to attract visitors over the long term.

➢Paid advertising

Social network advertising :

- Use the advertising options on Facebook, Instagram, Twitter, and LinkedIn to promote your blog posts to your target audience.

Google Ads :

- Create pay-per-click (PPC) advertising campaigns on Google to drive visitors to specific blog posts.

Chapter 7: Monetizing your blog

Monetizing a blog can be done in many different ways, and the best method often depends on the nature of your blog, your audience, and your skills. Here's a comprehensive guide to the different ways of monetizing a blog, as well as advice on choosing the best strategy for you :

➢Display ads

Google AdSense :

- Advantages: Easy to set up, no sales requirements.
- Disadvantages: Variable and often low revenues for small blogs.
- Tips: Make sure your blog generates enough traffic to maximize revenue. Place ads in strategic locations without detracting from the user experience.

Ad networks :

- Advantages: Personalization options and payout rates often higher than Google AdSense.
- Disadvantages: Traffic requirements may be higher.
- Tips: Look for ad networks that are tailored to your niche, such as Mediavine or AdThrive.

➢Affiliate marketing

Affiliate programs :

- Advantages: High passive income potential, flexibility.
- Disadvantages: Requires transparency and trust with your audience.
- Tips: Join affiliate programs relevant to your niche, such as Amazon Associates, ShareASale, or Commission Junction. Integrate affiliate links naturally into your content.

Affiliate marketing is a popular monetization method for bloggers and content creators. It involves promoting products or services from other companies and earning a commission on every sale or action made as a result of your referrals. Here's a complete guide to affiliate marketing:

➢Understanding affiliate marketing

- You sign up for an affiliate program offered by a company.
- The company provides you with unique affiliate links that you can use to promote their products or services.
- When someone clicks on your link and performs an action (purchase, registration, etc.), you earn a commission.

➢Choosing the right affiliate programs

Search for programs :

- Amazon Associates :
One of the largest affiliate programs, offering a wide range of products.
- ShareASale :
A platform for thousands of affiliate programs in various niches.
- Commission Junction (CJ) :
Another well-established affiliate network with numerous partners.
- Awin :
Offers affiliate programs in several sectors, including retail and financial services.
Selection criteria :
- Relevance: Choose products or services relevant to your audience.
- Commission: Compare commission rates and payment structures.
- Reliability: Select affiliate programs with good reviews and a solid reputation.

➢Integrating affiliate links

Strategic placement :

- Blog posts: Include affiliate links in relevant blog posts, such as product reviews, buying guides or advice articles.

- Banners and widgets: Use banner ads and widgets on your blog to promote products.

- Resource lists: Create pages dedicated to recommended resources, with affiliate links to the products and services you use and recommend.

Engaging content :

- Reviews and testimonials: Write honest, detailed reviews of the products or services you recommend.

- Tutorials and guides: Create tutorials or how-to guides that incorporate affiliate links in a natural way.

- Comparisons: Compare different products or services and use affiliate links for each one.

➢Digital products and services

E-books and guides :

- Advantages: Full control over product and pricing, high revenue per sale.
- Disadvantages: Time and effort required to create the product.
- Tips: Identify your audience's needs and create products that meet them. Use your blog to promote and sell your products.

Online courses and webinars :

- Advantages: Potentially high revenues, authority in your field.
- Disadvantages: Requires content creation and marketing skills.
- Tips: Use platforms like Teachable, Udemy, or Kajabi to host your courses.

Promote them via your blog and social networks.

➢Services

Consultancy and coaching :

- Advantages: High income, opportunities to build personalized relationships.
- Disadvantages: Requires time and personal commitment.
- Tips: Offer consulting or coaching services in your area of expertise.

➢Develop an effective monetization strategy

This is a crucial aspect that requires a structured and thoughtful approach. Here are the key steps to get you started:

➢Define your objectives

Clarity of objectives :

- Determine what you want to achieve with monetizing your blog (additional income, full-time income replacement, brand expansion, etc.).
- Set goals that are specific, measurable, achievable, relevant and time-bound (SMART).

➢Know your audience

Audience analysis :

- Use analytics tools (Google Analytics, etc.) to understand your audience's demographics, interests and behaviors.
- Identify your audience's needs and issues to better target products or services that will be useful to them.

Segmentation :

- Segment your audience into distinct groups based on their interests and behavior.
- Tailor your monetization strategy to these segments to maximize relevance and effectiveness.

➢Choosing the right monetization methods

Evaluate options :

- Evaluate the different monetization methods outlined above according to your niche and audience.

Combining methods :

- Often, a combination of several monetization methods is more effective than a single method.
- For example, you can use display advertising while doing affiliate marketing and selling digital products.

➢Creating quality, optimized content

Strategic content :
- Create specific types of content for monetization, such as product reviews, buying guides, comparisons, tutorials, etc.

➢Integrate monetization methods into your content

Affiliate links :

- Integrate affiliate links into your articles in a natural and relevant way.
- Use calls to action to encourage clicks and conversions.

Advertising :

- Place ads in strategic locations on your site without detracting from the user experience.
- Experiment with different ad formats to see what works best.

➤Mistakes to avoid when monetizing

Monetizing a blog can be very lucrative, but there are several common mistakes that bloggers often make, which can hinder their success. Here's a list of the most common mistakes to avoid:

1. Rushing into monetization

Mistake :
- Monetize too early before you have a sufficient audience.

Consequence :
- Reduced audience trust and engagement if you seem too focused on financial gain from the start.

Solution :
- Focus first on creating quality content and building a loyal audience. Wait until you have a steady stream of visitors before introducing monetization strategies.

2. Choosing irrelevant products

Mistake :
- Promoting products or services that aren't relevant to your audience.

Consequence :
- Loss of audience trust and low conversion rate.

Solution :
- Choose products or services that match your audience's interests and needs. Make sure you test or know the products well before recommending them.

3. Lack of transparency

Mistake :
- Not disclosing affiliate partnerships or sponsored content.

Consequence :
- Loss of credibility and trust from your audience, even legal problems.

Solution :
- Be transparent with your readers by clearly disclosing when you use affiliate links or publish sponsored content.

4. Advertising overload

Mistake :
- Filling your blog with too many ads.

Consequence :
- Poor user experience, which can lead to lower traffic and revenue in the long term.

Solution :
- Use ads strategically, placing them in non-intrusive locations. Focus on the user experience while balancing ad placements.

5. Neglect SEO

Mistake :
- Not optimizing your blog for search engines.

Consequence :
- Decreased organic traffic, which reduces monetization opportunities.

Solution :
- Invest time in SEO (keyword optimization, quality content creation, backlinks, etc.) to improve your blog's visibility in search engines.

6. Poor expectation management

Mistake :
- Expecting quick and significant results without sustained effort.

Consequence :
- Frustration and premature abandonment of monetization strategies. Many bloggers think they can make money quickly without understanding the time and effort required to build a successful blog.

Solution :
- Patience and perseverance: Understand that building a profitable blog takes time. Significant income usually comes only after creating lots of quality content and building a loyal audience.
- Set realistic goals: Break down your goals into small, achievable steps. For example, instead of aiming for €1,000 a month from the outset, aim first for €100, then €500, and so on.
- Consistency: Be consistent in your content creation and promotional efforts. Regularity is key to attracting and retaining an audience.
- Ongoing training: Keep abreast of best practices and new monetization strategies. The blogging world evolves rapidly, and it's important to adapt and learn continuously.

➢Here's an example of managing expectations

Let's say you're launching a travel blog. Here's how you might manage your expectations:

1.   First 3 months :
- Goal: Create 20 quality articles.
- Monetization: Add basic affiliate links and some advertising.
- Expectations: Expect little or no revenue, focus on content creation and SEO.

2. 6-12 months :
- Objective: Increase organic traffic by optimizing SEO and guest blogging.
- Monetization: Test different affiliate programs and advertising formats.
- Expectations: Start seeing some modest income, understand what works best for your audience.

3. 1-2 years :
- Goal: Build a list of newsletter subscribers, diversify monetization methods (e-books, online courses).
- Monetization: Introduce digital products and services, negotiate sponsored partnerships.
- Expectations: Achieve stable and growing income, increase audience engagement.

➢Conclusion :
Having realistic expectations, and managing those expectations with patience and perseverance, is crucial to successful blog monetization. The key is to stay focused on long-term growth, be consistent in your efforts and always seek to learn and improve your strategies.

Chapter 8: Managing and developing your blog

Here are some tips for managing and evolving your blog to ensure its continued success and growth :

1. Planning and organization

Establish an editorial calendar :
- Plan your content in advance by creating an editorial calendar. This will help you stay organized and publish regularly.
- Include dates for researching, writing, proofreading and publishing articles.

Diversify your content :
- Vary the type of content: blog posts, videos, infographics, podcasts, etc.
- Try out different formats and topics to see what resonates best with your audience.

2. Audience engagement

Interact with your readers :
- Respond to comments on your blog and on your social networks.
- Ask questions at the end of your articles to encourage discussion.
- Organize polls or surveys to get feedback and suggestions from your readers.

Create a community :
- Consider creating a Facebook group or discussion forum where your readers can interact with each other and with you.
- Use a newsletter to stay in regular contact with your subscribers and provide them with exclusive content.

3. Ongoing optimization

Performance analysis :
- Use Google Analytics and other tools to track your blog's performance (traffic, bounce rate, time spent on site, etc.).
- Analyze which articles are performing best and identify the reasons for their success.

SEO (Search Engine Optimization) :
- Continue to optimize your articles for search engines by using relevant keywords, alt tags for images, and internal links.
- Follow SEO trends and adjust your strategy accordingly.

4. Growth and expansion

Collaborations and partnerships :
- Collaborate with other bloggers, influencers or brands in your niche for content exchanges, interviews or joint campaigns.
- Participate in online or physical events to expand your network and attract new readers.

Diversify traffic sources :
- Use social networks, email marketing, forums and other platforms to drive traffic to your blog.
- Experiment with paid advertising campaigns if your budget allows.

5. Monetization and revenue

Diversify monetization methods :
- Don't hesitate to test different monetization methods (affiliate marketing, digital products, services, subscriptions, etc.).
- Monitor the performance of each method and adjust accordingly.

Offer quality products/services :
- If you sell products or services, make sure they bring real value to your readers.
- Collect customer feedback and use it to continually improve your offerings.

6. Continuous training and adaptation

Stay informed :
- Keep up to date with industry trends, new technologies and blogging best practices.
- Attend webinars, read books, and take online courses to improve your skills.

Be flexible and adaptable :
- Be prepared to adjust your strategy based on feedback from your audience.

Of course, here are even more detailed tips for managing and evolving your blog, covering additional aspects such as financial management, online reputation management and continuous improvement :

7. Financial management

Track income and expenses :
- Keep a detailed record of all your sources of income and expenses related to the blog (hosting, tools, advertising, etc.).
- Use accounting software to simplify financial management and generate accurate reports.

Strategic investment :
- Reinvest a portion of your revenue in tools, training and services that can improve the quality and reach of your blog.
- Prioritize investments that offer a high return on investment, such as advanced SEO courses or powerful analytics tools.

8. Online reputation management

Brand monitoring :
- Use tools like Google Alerts to monitor mentions of your blog and name on the Internet.
- Respond quickly and professionally to comments and reviews, whether positive or negative.

Build a strong brand image :
- Develop a consistent visual identity (logo, color palette, typography) and use it across all your channels.
- Communicate transparently and authentically to build trust with your audience.

9. Continuous improvement

Collect feedback :
- Regularly solicit feedback from your audience through surveys, questionnaires or comments.
- Analyze this feedback to identify areas for improvement and new content opportunities.

Competitor analysis :
- Monitor competitor blogs to understand what works in your niche and what you can improve or differentiate on your own blog.
- Adopt the best practices you observe while maintaining your own unique voice and style.

10. Innovation and adaptation

Test and experiment :
- Don't be afraid to try out new ideas, formats or technologies. Test different approaches to see what resonates best with your audience.
- Use A/B testing to evaluate the effectiveness of your content, design and monetization strategies.

Trend tracking :
- Stay up-to-date with emerging trends in blogging and your specific niche.
- Adapt your strategies quickly to take advantage of new opportunities before your competitors do.

11. Technical optimization

Site performance :
- Make sure your site loads quickly and is technically optimized. Use tools like Google PageSpeed Insights to identify and correct performance problems.
- Use quality hosting and optimize images and other resources to reduce loading times.

Site security :
- Protect your site against online threats by using security plugins, SSL certificates and regular backups.
- Update your blog platform and plugins regularly to avoid vulnerabilities.

12. Personal development and training

Continuing education :
- Invest in online courses, webinars and conferences to improve your skills in copywriting, SEO, digital marketing, etc.
- Read books and follow well-known bloggers and experts to stay inspired and informed.

Networking and mentoring :
- Participate in blogger groups, forums and events to exchange ideas and tips.
- Find a mentor or join communities where you can learn from the experiences of others.

13. Adapting to change

Flexibility and resilience :
- Be prepared to adapt your strategies as search algorithms, social media platforms and audience behaviors change.
- Develop contingency plans to deal with the unexpected, such as traffic drops or regulatory changes.

Constant innovation :
- Continually look for ways to innovate, whether through new content formats, creative collaborations or emerging technologies like AI or augmented reality.

➤ Conclusion :

Managing and evolving a blog is a dynamic and complex process. By combining rigorous planning, continuous adaptation to trends, technical optimization and effective reputation and financial management, you can create a resilient and successful blog. Lasting success depends on the ability to innovate, to learn constantly and to adapt to changes in the market and your audience's expectations.

Chapter 9: Overcoming obstacles

Overcoming criticism, negative feedback and lack of motivation is crucial to the long-term success of your blog. Here are a few tips to help you manage these challenges:

➢ **Dealing with criticism and negative comments**

1.   Adopt a constructive attitude

- Listen and analyze: Take the time to read reviews carefully to see if they contain valid points that could help you improve your blog.
- Respond politely: Respond courteously and professionally, even if the comments are negative. Thank them for their feedback and, if possible, explain how you plan to improve the criticized aspects.

2.   Developing a thick skin

- Accept criticism: Understand that receiving criticism is part of the growth process. Not everyone will agree with you or like your content.
- Don't take criticism personally: Try not to let criticism get to you emotionally. Concentrate on the constructive aspects and ignore purely negative or malicious comments.

3.   Filter comments

- Moderation: Use moderation tools to filter out abusive or inappropriate comments. Set clear rules for comments on your blog.
- Comment policy: Establish and communicate a comment policy that encourages respectful and constructive discussion.

➢ Overcoming lack of motivation

1. Set clear, achievable goals

- Short-term goals: Break down your long-term goals into smaller, achievable steps. This will give you a sense of achievement and keep you motivated.
- Track progress: Use tools to track your progress and celebrate small victories along the way.

2. Stay inspired

- Consume inspirational content: Read blogs, books, listen to podcasts or watch videos by creators you admire to stay inspired.
- Vary your activities: Change your routine by trying out new writing techniques or content formats.

3. Create a positive work environment

- Dedicated workspace: Set up a comfortable and inspiring workspace. A pleasant environment can improve your concentration and motivation.
- Time management: Use time management techniques such as the Pomodoro method to structure your work sessions and avoid procrastination.

4. Taking care of yourself

- Regular breaks: Give yourself regular breaks to avoid overwork. Exercising, meditating or simply relaxing can help recharge your batteries.
- Work/life balance: Balance your work on the blog with other aspects of your life. Having a balanced life helps maintain motivation in the long term.

5. Find support

- Community: Join blogging communities where you can share experiences, ask for advice and get support.
- Mentoring: Find a mentor or colleague with whom you can discuss your challenges and get practical advice.

➢ Why is a long-term vision important?

1. Ongoing motivation :

- Focus and clarity: A long-term vision gives you a clear direction and a goal to aim for. This can help you stay motivated, even during periods of discouragement.
- Sense of progress: With a long-term perspective, you can better appreciate the small steps and progress you've made, which boosts your motivation.

2. Strategic decision-making :

- Alignment of actions: A long-term vision enables you to align your daily actions with your ultimate goals, ensuring that every effort contributes to your overall success.
- Priority management: This helps you prioritize your tasks and focus your resources on what's really important to achieve your long-term goals.

3. Resilience in the face of challenges :

- Perseverance: A long-term vision helps you overcome temporary obstacles by reminding you that challenges are part of the process and that success takes time.
- Adaptability: With a long-term perspective, you're better prepared to adjust your strategies in line with market developments and audience feedback.

➢ How to maintain a long-term vision?

1. Define clear, measurable objectives :

- SMART objectives: set objectives that are specific, measurable, achievable, relevant and time-bound. For example, "Reach 10,000 monthly visitors by the end of the year" or "Generate $500 in monthly affiliate revenue in six months".
- Break down into steps: Break these goals down into smaller, more manageable steps. This makes ambitious goals less daunting and more attainable.

2.   Create a roadmap :

- Long-term plan: Develop a roadmap that details the steps needed to reach your long-term goals. Include important milestones and target dates.
- Flexibility: Be ready to adjust your roadmap according to market developments and audience feedback.

3.   Evaluate and adjust regularly :

- Periodic reviews: Schedule quarterly or semi-annual reviews to assess your progress against your long-term goals. Identify what's working and what needs adjustment.
- Feedback and adaptation: Solicit feedback from your audience and use it to refine your strategies. Be flexible and open to necessary changes.

4.   Visualization and affirmation :

- Vision board: Create a vision board with images and words that represent your long-term goals. Place it in a visible place so you're constantly reminded of your aspirations.
- Positive affirmations: Use positive affirmations to reinforce your commitment to your goals. For example, "I am capable of creating a successful blog and achieving my goals."

5.   Balance between short term and long term :

- Daily actions aligned: Make sure your daily actions and short-term decisions are aligned with your long-term vision.
- Short-term rewards: Celebrate small victories along the way to keep you motivated while keeping an eye on your long-term goals.

➤ Conclusion

Dealing with criticism and lack of motivation is essential to maintaining a thriving blog. Adopt a constructive attitude to criticism, set clear and achievable goals, stay inspired and surround yourself with support. By taking care of yourself and creating a positive working environment, you'll be better prepared to overcome obstacles and keep moving forward with your blog. What's more, maintaining a long-term vision is essential to navigating challenges and staying on course for success. By creating a roadmap, regularly evaluating your progress and remaining flexible, you can ensure the growth and sustainability of your blog. A long-term vision helps you stay motivated, make strategic decisions and persevere in the face of obstacles, while adapting to the changes needed to achieve your goals.

Chapter 10: Conclusion

Summary of key points for a successful blog

If you manage to tick most of the boxes relating to the items listed below, you're seriously on the road to success.

➤ **Don't give up, and be patient!**

1.   Define a long-term vision

- Set clear, measurable objectives.
- Create a detailed roadmap with milestones.
- Regularly review and adjust your plan based on results and feedback.

2.   Choose the right platform and domain name

- Select a platform suited to your needs (WordPress, Wix, Webador, etc.).
- Choose a domain name that's memorable, easy to spell and representative of your niche.

3.   Find the right niche

- Identify an area that you're passionate about and that has a potential audience.
- Conduct a market analysis to understand competition and opportunities.

4.   Create Quality Content

- Draw up an editorial calendar to organize and plan your publications.
- Vary the types of content (articles, videos, infographics) to keep your readers interested.
- Provide useful, well-researched and engaging information.

5. Search Engine Optimization (SEO)

- Use relevant keywords and optimize title tags, descriptions and images.
- Create internal and external links to enhance your blog's authority.
- Make sure your site is fast and mobile-friendly.

6. Audience promotion and engagement

- Use social networks to share your content and interact with your audience.
- Set up a newsletter to retain your readers and offer them exclusive content.
- Participate in forums and online groups related to your niche.

7. Monetize

- Diversify your sources of income: affiliate marketing, advertising, digital products, services.
- Offer quality products or services that add value to your audience.
- Develop a long-term monetization strategy and track your performance.

8. Analysis and Continuous Improvement

- Use analytics tools like Google Analytics to track your performance.
- Gather feedback from your audience to continually improve your content and offers.
- Keep abreast of trends and best practices in your niche.

9. Criticism and Negative Comment Management

- Respond to criticism constructively and professionally.
- Use criticism to identify areas for improvement.
- Moderate comments to maintain a positive and respectful environment.

10. Maintaining motivation

- Set short- and long-term goals to keep you motivated.
- Vary your activities and look for sources of inspiration to stay creative.
- Take care of yourself and find a balance between work and personal life.

11. Technical and security management

- Make sure your site loads quickly and is technically optimized.
- Protect your blog with appropriate security measures, such as SSL certificates and regular backups.

12. Adaptation and Innovation

- Be flexible and ready to adapt your strategies in line with market developments and audience feedback.
- Experiment with new ideas, formats and technologies to keep your blog fresh and relevant.

➢ Encouragement and advice for the future.

Starting a blog is an exciting and rewarding adventure that can open many doors, both personally and professionally. Here are some words of encouragement and advice to help you persevere with your project :

1.   Believe in yourself and your vision

- You have a unique perspective and stories to tell. Believe in the value of what you have to offer. Every great blogger started somewhere, and with hard work and determination, you can succeed too.

2.   Perseverance pays off

- Success in blogging doesn't come overnight. There will be ups and downs, but every step is a learning opportunity. Keep moving forward, even when results seem slow in coming.

3.   Your voice counts

- No matter how many blogs exist, no one has your voice. Your authenticity and passion can create a deep connection with your audience.

4.   Celebrate every little victory

- Whether it's a new comment, a share on social networks or an increase in traffic, every little success deserves to be celebrated. These moments are indicators of your progress.

➤A few tips for the future :

1.   Start with solid planning

- Establish a clear vision for your blog and define short- and long-term goals. A well-thought-out plan will guide you and help you stay focused.

2.   Be yourself

- Authenticity is key. Write about things you're passionate about, and express yourself honestly. Readers are drawn to authentic, passionate voices.

3.   Learn and evolve constantly

- The blogging world is constantly evolving. Keep learning new techniques, following trends and improving your skills. Invest in your education through courses, books and webinars.

4.   Engage with your audience

- Take the time to respond to comments, interact on social networks and build a community around your blog. Engaging with your readers builds loyalty and enriches your blogging experience.

5.   Be patient and persistent

- Growth takes time. Be patient and persistent, even when progress seems slow. Every effort counts and contributes to your long-term success.

6.   Don't be afraid of failure

- Mistakes and failures are part of the process. Learn from each experience and use these lessons to improve. Obstacles are opportunities in disguise.

7.   Optimize and promote assiduously

- Publish quality content regularly and optimize it for search engines (SEO). Use social networks, newsletters and other channels to promote your blog and attract new readers.

8.   Take care of yourself

- Blogging can be demanding. Make sure you take care of your mental and physical well-being. A good work-life balance is essential to keep you motivated and creative.

➢Conclusion

Successful blogging relies on a combination of strategic vision, quality content, technical optimization, audience engagement and revenue diversification. By following these key points and remaining adaptable and persistent, you can create and maintain a successful and sustainable blog.

Getting into blogging is an exciting adventure full of possibilities. With passion, patience and perseverance, you can create a blog that not only reflects your vision, but also resonates with a wide audience. Believe in yourself, stay authentic and keep learning and evolving. The journey can be difficult, but it's also incredibly rewarding.

Good luck and, above all, happy blogging!

To you, my children, Jérémy and Chloé...

I love you!

Blurb Editions is committed to preserving the
environment by reducing the carbon footprint of its
books through the use of certified fiber-based paper.

Printed on Blurb Inc. presses in October 2024.

www.ingramcontent.com/pod-product-compliance
Lightning Source LLC
LaVergne TN
LVHW051748050326
832903LV00029B/2798